Buffalo Music

by Tracey E. Fern

Illustrated by Lauren Castillo

CLARION BOOKS ❦ NEW YORK

When I first settled here, hard on the rim of Palo Duro Canyon, I had no company but for the animals. I woke to the reveille of the roosters. I did chores to the choir of the crows. I dreamed to the chorus of the coyotes. Mostly, though, I lived to the music of the buffalo.

I stirred the fire to the *huff-huff* of buffalo breath clouding the chill dawn.

I hoed the garden to the *scritch-scritch* of buffalo scratching themselves against the cottonwoods.

I scrubbed the bedclothes to the slosh and splash of buffalo bulls wallowing in the mud hole.

I swept the dugout to the thunder of buffalo as they drifted like a dark cloud across the prairie.

Buffalo are homely, feisty critters with a stubborn streak wider than the Rio Grande. My husband, Charlie, says they remind me of my own self and that's why I have such a fondness for them. 'Course, I can't argue with him, for fear of proving him right. But no matter the why or wherefore, that buffalo music played right to my heart.

One day different sounds filled the canyon—the boom and blast of rifles.

"What are all them shots?" I asked Charlie.

"Buffalo hunters, Molly," he said. "Fixin' to turn a profit on hides and hooves."

Seemed like every man in Texas was afire to make a fortune in the buffalo business.
Day after day, the hunters galloped into the heart of the herd. Shots echoed over the hills
and through the hollows from sunup till sundown. And day after day, another hundred
or more buffalo lay dead.

The heat that summer fell heavy as an angry fist. The trails were deep with dust.
The grass cracked like glass underfoot. And everywhere, far as the eye could see,
the bleached bones of the buffalo glistened white in the sun.

"How many till they've killed enough?" I asked Charlie as we rode by a mountain of buffalo skulls, tall as ten men.

"Guess they figure no matter how many they kill, there's enough to roam these plains forever," Charlie said.

But forever came fast. Within six seasons, the hunters were gone. So was the buffalo music.

Oh, those were lonely, silent days! I was near sure the only song left in the canyon was the cold whistle of the north wind.

But one spring morning, I was lugging wash water up from the river when a cowhand name of Billie came trotting up.

"Howdy, Miss Molly," Billie said. "Got some orphans for you."

Billie knew I had a soft spot for critters. He'd bring me whatever stray or sickly creature he found on the trail—prairie dogs, wolf pups, wild turkeys. Once even an antelope.

"What did you bring this time?" I asked Billie as I set down the water and went to have a look.

Two buffalo calves were trailing after him, skinny as hungry snakes.

"Found 'em snoozin' under a juniper," Billie said. "Hunters must've figured they were too puny to fuss with. Think you can fatten 'em up?"

Right then one of the calves let out a soft snort. Lordy, that sound brought back some memories! I didn't need to hear anything else afore making up my mind.

"Can't tell till I try," I told Billie. "Let's get 'em inside before they're supper for the wolves."

I know some people think I'm tough as old beef jerky, but truth is, I'd seen too many living things disappear in the hard struggle for life here. I wasn't about to let the buffalo go, too.

Now, mind you, I don't look a thing like a buffalo mama. I'm thin as a flapjack and not much taller, but those calves up and followed me back to the dugout, strolled in through the front door, and set down in front of the fire!

I named one Calico, seeing as she was the same faded red as my favorite dress. I called the other Chester, after a neighbor back home in Tennessee with the same fierce-eyed stare.

Then I set to work tending them. I tucked hot-water bottles inside flannel cloth and wrapped a cloth around each calf like swaddling around a babe. I fed them like babes, too, squeezing cow's milk from a rag.

They took to it like flies to a keg of molasses. Lordy, those two could drink—three gallons a day or more! Kept me so busy, I hardly had time to blink.

Charlie just shook his head at me, like I didn't have enough brains to grease a skillet. "Buffalo aren't long for this land," he told me. "Tending to those two runts won't change that."

But Charlie knew better than to waste his breath arguing with me. When I got a notion, a wise man knew to let me have my way. And I'd got a notion that I was going to hear buffalo music again in this lifetime.

Within a few weeks, Calico and Chester were plump as biscuit dumplings! By then, Charlie had had his fill of wild critters in the dugout. He fenced off a section of pasture, and I turned the calves loose with the milking cows.

At first, the cows showed their hind ends to Calico and Chester. Then they tried to butt them out of the herd. But I didn't give them a choice. I snubbed those buffalo up tight to two cows until the cows finally came around and started nursing them like the calves were their own. By the time winter set in, them calves had a good inch of horn, a fine woolly beard, and the strength to turn Charlie's fences into kindling wood!

Pretty soon, word got out all over the Panhandle that I was tending buffalo calves. Every time a cowhand rode up with another orphan, Charlie'd heave a sigh and start stoking the dugout fire.

Maybe he was right—the wild herds likely were long gone, disappeared like dew before the sun. But I knew there was another way to end the silence in the canyon: start a herd of my own.

I set to work feeding and watering my orphans, mending the sick, breeding the healthy, and fending off wolves and poachers with the long end of my rifle.

With time and tending, my little herd grew. Soon I had one hundred head.

Then one day, word came that Yellowstone National Park was looking
to rebuild its buffalo herd. Soon as I heard that, I got to work.

I drove Calico and Chester and two yearlings to the east edge of our spread, where the Santa Fe line came through. I set Billie to work building four timber stalls spiked to the frame of a boxcar. We fastened up some thick padding to keep the buffalo safe from the swaying and jostling of the train. Then I loaded up the boxcar with bales of hay and barrels of water.

"How are we going to get them onboard?" Billie asked, gathering his rope and eyeing the bulls' horns. "They could bust through that boxcar as easy as one of Charlie's fences."

I didn't have to think on it too long. I just took a lesson from how Charlie treats me when I'm feeling ornery and let them have their own way.

"Drop your rope," I told Billie. Then I tucked a chunk of molasses cake in my apron, walked slowly past the buffalo, and waited in the boxcar. Few minutes later, when they were good and ready, all four just strolled up the ramp after me, gentle as newborn lambs.

I couldn't leave the rest of my herd. Billie would tend these four till they got settled on their new range. "Take good care of my babes," I told him as he climbed aboard and the brakeman hitched the car to the next through freight train.

I stood watching till the last pale wake of smoke whisked away in the wind, till the last hollow echo of the train whistle faded.

"Good luck to you, my old friends," I whispered.

When Billie wrote a few months later, he had some big news. Calico had birthed a healthy calf. Lordy, that was some day! To my way of thinking, it wasn't just the birth of a calf—it was the rebirth of our national herd.

The sounds of the canyon are different now. Settlers have crowded in. Fences and longhorns dot the land as far as the eye can see. Nowadays, I wake to the rumble of engines, do chores to the whoop and holler of a hundred cowhands, and go to sleep to the blast of the train whistles.

But some days when I ride north beyond the last stand of salt cedar, I can once again hear the faint chords of the old songs. I hear the clatter of clashing horns. I hear the bellowing of the bulls. I hear the muffled thud of hooves as they hurl up dust. And I live on the keen edge of hope that one day the strains of that sweet, wild music will echo far beyond these canyon walls.

Clarion Books • a Houghton Mifflin Company imprint • 215 Park Avenue South, New York, NY 10003 • Text copyright © 2008 by Tracey E. Fern
Illustrations copyright © 2008 by Lauren Castillo • The illustrations were executed in mixed media. • The text was set in 15-point Old Claude LP.
All rights reserved. • For information about permission to reproduce selections from this book, write to Permissions, Houghton Mifflin Company,
215 Park Avenue South, New York, NY 10003. • www.clarionbooks.com • Printed in Singapore • Library of Congress Cataloging-in-Publication Data
Fern, Tracey E. • Buffalo music / by Tracey Fern ; [illustrated by Lauren Castillo]. • p. cm. • Summary: After hunters kill off the buffalo around her
Texas ranch, a woman begins raising orphan buffalo calves and eventually ships four members of her small herd to Yellowstone National Park, where
they form the beginnings of newly thriving buffalo herds. Based on the true story of Mary Ann Goodnight and her husband Charles.
ISBN 0-618-72341-2 • [1. American bison—Fiction. 2. Goodnight, Mary Ann, d. 1926—Fiction. 3. Texas—Fiction.] I. Castillo, Lauren, ill. II. Title.
PZ7.F3589Bu 2008 • [E]—dc22 • 2007018435 • ISBN-13: 978-0-618-72341-6
TWP 10 9 8 7 6 5 4 3 2 1

AUTHOR'S NOTE

This is a work of fiction, but it was inspired by real events. In particular, the character of Molly is based on Mary Ann Goodnight, a pioneer who settled in the Palo Duro Canyon in 1876. At that time, enormous herds of buffalo still roamed West Texas. Within a few years, hunters had slaughtered nearly every one.

Mary Ann Goodnight and her husband, Charles, were some of the first people to recognize the need to save the species from extinction. They adopted several orphan buffalo calves and slowly began to build a captive herd. Soon a few other ranchers in the West, including James McKay, Charles Alloway, Samuel Walking Coyote, Frederic Dupree, and Charles "Buffalo" Jones, also began to capture and breed buffalo.

Mary Ann's buffalo herd formed one of five foundation herds in the United States from which most of the current herds have been bred. She shipped four buffalo to Yellowstone National Park in 1896 under the care of a cowboy named William Timmons. At the time, there were fewer than fifty buffalo in the park. She later sent more buffalo to Yellowstone, as well as some to the Wichita Mountains Wildlife Refuge in Oklahoma, the National Bison Range in Montana, and several zoos. Thanks to conservationists like Mary Ann, if you listen hard enough, you can still hear the faint sounds of buffalo music echo across the plains of North America.

If you would like to learn more about the buffalo, there are many excellent books for young readers. *Saving the Buffalo* by Albert Marrin (New York: Scholastic, 2006) contains general information on the buffalo, as well as information about their near extinction and efforts to save them. *Thunder on the Plains: The Story of the American Buffalo* by Ken Robbins (New York: Atheneum Books for Young Readers, 2001) is an overview of the slaughter of the buffalo. *American Bison* by Ruth Berman (Minneapolis, Minn.: Carolrhoda Books, 1992) contains useful information about the life cycle and habits of the buffalo. *The Buffalo and the Indians: A Shared Destiny* by Dorothy Hinshaw Patent (New York: Clarion Books, 2006) describes the importance of the buffalo to Native American cultures. In addition, the webcast "Challenge at Caprock: Saving the Bison," located at http://www.tpwd.state.tx.us/learning/webcasts/bison, and in particular its resources page, contains a wealth of information about buffalo, the Goodnights, and the Texas Panhandle and its history. Finally, *The Handbook of Texas Online,* located on the Texas State Historical Association Online website at www.tsha.utexas.edu is a searchable database full of helpful information that can be accessed by searching such terms as "Goodnight, Mary Ann Dyer," "Goodnight Ranch," "Goodnight, Charles," "buffalo hunting," "buffalo," and "Palo Duro Canyon."

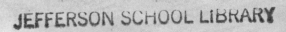